ISLE *of* WIGHT

IN OLD PHOTOGRAPHS

ISLAND BOOKS
NEWPORT, ISLE OF WIGHT

Isle of Wight in Old Photographs
© 1994
Island Books

Island Books is an imprint of Ravenswood Publications, London

Distributed by HBS, Newport, Isle of Wight

Printed and bound by Crossprint Limited, Newport, Isle of Wight

ISBN 1 898198 02 0

RYDE FROM THE PIER.

Having enjoyed a breezy trip across the Solent, we arrive at our starting place, Ryde Pier, which was erected in 1814, and is nearly half a mile in length. Worthy of note is the Electric Tramway adjoining, which, for the moderate charge of one penny, carries us to the end of the Pier. The Railway Companies built the iron pier to the east of it in 1879. At the Pier Head is a fine Pavilion, commanding a good view of the town, also of the yacht racing which takes place in the Solent every summer.

Leaving the Pier we reach the

Esplanade, where we may make our choice of visiting any part of the Island by Train, Tally-Ho, or Motor Car. The Esplanade which was built in 1865, is nearly a mile long, having been extended in 1881 so as to include a beautifully wooded footpath at its eastern extremity known as Appley Walk. The Gardens are neatly laid out and possess a Band Stand. The Canoe Lake is the centre of much attraction for not only are model yachts sailed here, but you may "paddle your own canoe," which is more than can be said of many other model lakes. A favourite walk is along the sea front to Sea View, about two miles. Ryde has a population of 12,000.

QUARR ABBEY.

RYDE ESPLANADE.

APPLEY WATCH TOWER.

THE WESTERN ESPLANADE IS QUITE NEW, HAVING ONLY RECENTLY BEEN RECLAIMED.

Leaving Ryde, and taking a westerly direction, starting by Spencer Road, which affords a good view over the Solent, then on the Newport Road a distance of two miles passing through Brinstead, brings us to Quarr Abbey, founded by Baldwin de Redvers, 1131.

HAZELWOOD, RYDE.

A Home of Rest and Recreation. It was purchased, enlarged, and put in trust, for the benefit of young men of the commercial class, by Sir George Williams, the honoured founder of the Young Men's Christian Association, in 1876 ; it was enlarged a second time in 1899. There is now accommodation for 100 visitors. It cost upwards of £13,000. This handsome building is situated about one mile from Ryde Pier, on high ground, and commands splendid views of both sea and land. The grounds belonging to the Home are extensive and well laid out. The interior is furnished in first-rate style and with refined taste. Its privileges are open to all commercial young men respectably introduced. From 1200 to 1300 visitors are received each year.

A distance of 2½ miles to the east of Ryde is Sea View, a bright little watering-place on Nettlestone Point. The surroundings are very pretty. A little inland are the well-timbered grounds of St. Clare, while southward the coast is picturesque with wood. It has of late become a very fashionable bathing-place.

Brading, 3½ miles from Ryde, in a southerly direction, with a population of 1500, consists of a single street. It is a place of ancient origin, having being probably occupied from the time of the Romans. The chief objects of interest are the Church at the top of the street, and the Roman Villa. In the ground of the open space half-way up the street is an iron ring, the old bull ring. Adjoining the churchyard is the Town Hall and Market House, and the old stocks and whipping-post are still preserved.

SANDOWN BAY

SANDOWN ESPLANADE

Sandown, with a population of 3593, is 2½ miles from Brading and 9¼ from Ryde. Its situation, on the open shore of Sandown Bay, gives it its distinctive character. The slope of the shore is gradual, and the sands good and extensive. The North end of the Bay is formed by the well-known Culver Cliffs, on the top of which is the Marconi Signalling Station. From these heights a grand view is obtained across the Bay to Dunnose.

Private and public enterprise have recently provided much for the comfort of visitors; a Kursaal has been erected, from which a grand view of the bay is obtained; while concert parties entertain you, and protected from the sun you enjoy a tête-à-tête over a cup of tea.

Overlooking the western end of the Esplanade are the beautiful pleasure grounds of Ferncliff (Admission, 1d.); these are easily approached by the rising zig-zag path from the Esplanade and no visitor should fail to pay them a visit. Abounding in sheltered nooks and shady paths, one can well spend a summer afternoon. Refreshments can be had at the House. Open air concerts are given at intervals.

SANDOWN LOOKING EAST.

Sandown has a fine Esplanade, which is well patronised, especially on a fine evening when the Band is playing ; this is one of the Chief Bathing Resorts in the Island.
Leaving the Esplanade a beautiful walk may be taken along the

ON THE CLIFFS AT SANDOWN

PARISH CHURCH SANDOWN

Cliffs; or, should it be preferred, the sands may be resorted to. From the cliff a fine view across the Channel is obtained, whilst, at the same time, we enjoy the beautiful country scenes which the Island so ably affords. About half-way between Sandown and Shanklin is the "Home of Rest," a fine block of buildings facing the sea. It was opened in 1893 by the Duke of Connaught.

A distance of 1½ miles brings us to

SHANKLIN PIER AND CLIFFS.

Shanklin. The Cliffs afford a delightful walk, with ever-varying view—a fresh swell from the English Channel on the one side, and the beautiful landscapes on the other. Compared with our busy towns, Shanklin is a haven of peace and quietness.

The Pier is a good one, and has lately been much improved, affording good accommodation for steamboats, which call daily during the season from various watering-places on the South Coast.

SHANKLIN (General View).

Shanklin is a town somewhat smaller than Sandown, having a population of 3500. The two places differ considerably, Sandown being a modern-built town, while Shanklin is an old and picturesque little village which has grown into a town. It is situated on a cliff about 130 feet above the sea, and directly under the cliff is the Esplanade

The Lift

HIGH St SHANKLIN

which may be reached by the winding road, by the lift, or through the chime.

   The Beach is a sandy one and is a fine resort for children; while being firm it affords good opportunity for sport both in and out of the sea, which is indulged in until 1 o'clock when everyone goes home to lunch, the weary ones patronising the lift; one of the chief features of interest is the Chine. It can be entered either from the beach at the south end of the Esplanade, or by the road at the top of the High Street, near the Crab Inn. It is a narrow gully in the green sand. A stream which flows through it forms a cascade at the head, and has doubtless been the principal agent in its formation. It is 450 feet long, and 250 feet wide at its mouth, which gradually diminishes to a few yards. The rocks on either side abound with all kinds of ferns, ivy, and moss, presenting a most refreshing appearance.

Midway through the Chine is a rustic stone bridge, quite in keeping with its surroundings.

SHANKLIN CHINE

THE STONE BRIDGE

THE OLD VILLAGE, SHANKLIN. I.W.

After leaving the Chine by the head, turning to the right, past the drinking fountain, we arrive at the Old Village, with the Crab Inn. The thatched roofs of the cottages, and quaint white fronts of the houses, present to us a glimpse of Shanklin in days gone by.

HOME OF REST
SHANKLIN

CHINE
ROAD

Old Shanklin Church

LUCCOMBE CHIN

An hour's walk along the seashore, when the tide is out, or about a mile over the cliffs, from Shanklin, we arrive at Luccombe Chine. The characteristics of this Chine are of a different description from those of Shanklin, and it is well worth a visit. Its chasm has been left in its natural state. The cliff path from Luccombe leads us through

IN THE LANDSLIP
VENTNOR

the Landslip, which is some 200 feet above the sea, but from 200 to 250 feet below verge of the cliff, which, in a rough chaos, bounds it landwards. The half-mile walk through the Landslip is charming. Small landslips in this vicinity are continually effecting changes in the surrounding scenery. Nature having adorned the ugly chasms, dells, and slopes with shrubs, ferns, and wild flowers, it is easy enough to lose one's way, unless a good look-out is kept for the path. After descending to within about forty feet of the shore, the path keeps near the sea cliff, coming out close to

BONCHURCH VALLEY.

the Valley of Bonchurch, situated to the east of Ventnor, to which it is so closely joined, formerly called Boneacre.   The village is situated in a valley, at the foot of St. Boniface Down.
The pond was formed from a swamp, which for generations supplied the materials for making the lobster pots for the fishermen of the village, who, until late years, were its only residents.

BONCHURCH CHURCH

The old Church, lower down the village, near the cliff, was founded about 1070, on the site of a still more ancient one. It is of Norman architecture. It has not been used for public service for many years. In the churchyard a feature worthy of notice is the tomb of the Rev. W. Adams, who laid the foundation stone of the new church and died the following year. It is surmounted by an iron cross, in order that the " Shadow of the Cross " may always fall upon the tomb.

THE VIADUCT

VENTNOR LOOKING WEST

Childrens Corner

The Pier, 650 feet long, is of the ordinary type, affording accommodation for steam-boats, which, during the summer, call with excursionists from all parts of the South Coast. From the Pier is afforded a fine view of the town and surrounding hills and cliffs. Coaches run to Blackgang all the year round (excepting Sundays), at the nominal charge of 1s. 6d. return. The Freshwater and other coaches run occasionally.

FROM THE PIER

STEEPHILL COVE

VENTNOR LOOKING EAST

Ventnor, built on the side of St. Boniface Down, a hill rising 800 feet above the sea. The houses rise terrace above terrace, all having a splendid outlook over the English Channel. The tourists will observe how the town is protected from the cold winds in the winter, and, facing south, enjoys the sunshine from morn till eve. The Pavilion on the Esplanade has recently been built, and was opened in 1896. It is much used as a social club; mostly built of glass, and contains a fine concert hall, capable of seating seven or eight hundred persons.

Steep Hill Cove, which may be seen from the Pier, is a pretty little nook, used almost exclusively by the fishermen, who may be seen busily employed mending nets and looking after their lobster pots.

VENTNOR CASCADE.

The Cascade is formed by the old Mill Stream which comes down Spring Hill and runs under Pier Street, formerly called Mill Street ; the stream some years ago drove a Mill which stood on the site of the Alexandra Gardens.

ROYAL NATIONAL HOSPITAL VENTNOR

Leaving Ventnor for Blackgang, distance 5½ miles, when about three-quarters of a mile on the road, we pass, on the left side, an extensive range of buildings. This is the National Hospital for Consumptive Patients, comprising eleven blocks, each semi-detached, the foundation stone of the last block having been laid in 1897 by Princess Henry of Battenburg. The houses all face due south, having a magnificent outlook across its extensive grounds to the English Channel.

ST CATHERINES
LIGHTHOUSE

CRIPPLE PATH

THE UNDERCLIFF

The Undercliff is an irregular cliff, here and there forming bays, caverns, and grottoes, where thick vegetation clings to the side of the cliffs. It is about six miles long, and varying in width from a quarter to half a mile. On the land side it is bounded by a cliff 200 feet in height, and presents to the sea a secondary cliff, which in places gives way to broken ground. After passing the Hospital, the old Church of St. Lawrence is reached, which, until the first Earl of Yarborough lengthened it, was the smallest parish church in England, it being 20 feet × 12 feet. It probably dates back to the twelfth century. Three miles from Ventnor is Cripple Path, which leads by zig-zags to the top of the cliff. About a mile further, and turning a little to the left, is St. Catherine's Lighthouse. The light is electric, being over 6,000,000 candle-power, and is visible for forty-two miles. Continuing on, past Sandrock Hotel and the Coastguard Station, we reach

BLACKGANG CHINE

Blackgang Chine. The usual approach is through the bazaar at the top. From the Observatory, on a clear day, the view is one of the best in the Island, the whole of the back of the Island being visible, and the Needles clearly seen. A path and steps lead down to the shore. A stream of water, which has its origin in a bed of sandstone, about 130 feet above the sea, falls 70 feet.

THE HOME OF THE DAIRYMAN'S DAUGHTER

GODSHILL CHURCH, I.W. STRUCK BY LIGHTNING, JAN. 14th, 1904.

ARRETON CHURCH, BURIAL PLACE OF THE DAIRYMAN'S DAUGHTER.

OLD CHURCH OF ST. LAWRANCE.

FRESHWATER ROCKS

TENNYSONS AVENUE

FRESHWATER BAY.

Freshwater Bay is one mile from Freshwater Railway Station. Before the arrival of the railway it was esteemed for its quiet isolation. Its magnificent chalk cliffs and downs, 483 feet high, afford fine rambling grounds. Bathing is good. Freshwater will ever be known by its long associations with the late Poet Laureate, Lord Tennyson. The grand arch is probably the finest natural arch on our shores, being 200 feet high.

NEEDLE ROCKS & LIGHT HOUSE FROM THE SOLENT

THE NEEDLE ROCKS

THE NEEDLES FROM END FORT

A walk of about two miles brings us to End Fort; directly above the Needles, from which a fine view of the rocks is secured. The land in this part is occupied by the War Department.

The Needle Rocks are formed from isolated masses of chalk, that, in consequence of their superior hardness, have survived the marine and atmospheric waste. They are situated at the west opening of the Solent.

ALUM BAY

NEEDLES & ALUM BAY

To the east of the Needles is Alum Bay. Here the white cliffs are succeeded by the well-known coloured sands. Thousands of visitors and excursionists come here from Southsea, Bournemouth, and other places on the mainland during the summer season.

The rapid succession of vertical layers of sand and clays of bright and varied hues produce a singular and beautiful effect. The central ridge, or backbone, consists of strata of chalk, embedding layers of flints and the underlying formations in an almost vertical position. When it is remembered that these beautiful sands once formed the bed of the ocean at this particular spot, the reader will have some idea of the great upheaval that must have taken place at an early period in the formation of this beautiful Island.

Headen Hall, which separates Alum Bay from

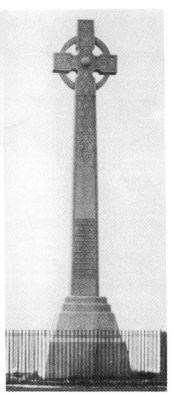

TENNYSON MEMORIAL CROSS,
FRESHWATER.

TOTLAND HOTEL

TOTLAND GENERAL
VIEW

PIER AND BEACH TOTLAND

Totland Bay, rises to a height of nearly 400 feet. Totland Bay is rapidly increasing in popularity; it is exceedingly healthy, being about 70 to 100 feet above the shore. It has a very fine hotel, which is replete with every comfort, situated on the top of the cliff. There is a Pier, at which excursion boats from different parts call daily. The commercial part of the place lies a little to the left. Bathing is good. Distance to Freshwater Railway Station about 1¼ miles, where train can be taken to the pretty and historic village of Carisbrooke, a distance of 11 miles.

CARISBROOKE VILLAGE

CASTLE STREET

Carisbrooke, though now a small village, was once the capital of the Island. The approach to Carisbrooke, with one of the most ancient castles in the United Kingdom towering above it, is exceedingly picturesque. The Village and Church, with its steeple and embattled towers, are prettily situated on the slope of a hill. The Church is one of the oldest in the Island, having been erected by William Fitz-Osborne in 1088. The remains of a Roman Villa were discovered in the garden of the Vicarage, 1859. It consists of several apartments, and its mosaic pavement is in good preservation.

Leaving the village by a steep road, we arrive at the

THE KEEP

THE DONKEY HOUSE

CARISBROOKE CASTLE

THE OLD GATE

Castle, which is the chief object of interest, notonly from its antiquity, but also its connection with Charles I. On entering the first object of interest is the Chapel of St. Nicholas, erected 1738, on the site of an older one. At one time it was customary for the Mayor of Newport to be sworn in in the Chapel, now a roofless ruin. On the other side are the ruins of the apartments occupied by Charles I. during his confinement here. The window through which the monarch attempted to escape is in existence. The most ancient portion of the Castle is the Keep. It is ascended by a flight of 74 steps, leading to a stout gateway, grooved by a portcullis. In the interior of this are 12 more steps, which lead to an irregular polygon, 60 feet broad, which is formed by the massive wall of the tower. The Well in the Keep is said to be 310 feet deep, but has long since been filled up. Leaving the Keep, we are taken across the Green to another well, which forms one of the greatest curiosities of the Island. Its depth is 144 feet, with 37 feet of water, which is drawn by a wheel turned by a donkey. The water is remarkable for its coolness

VICTORIA MONUMENT.

This Memorial was raised to the memory of the late Queen Victoria by the inhabitants of the Isle of Wight, and erected in the Market Place, Newport.

NEWPORT, FROM MOUNT JOY.

Leaving Carisbrooke and continuing our journey in a north-easterly direction, we arrive at Newport, the principal town (population 10,216), situated in the centre of the Island. It is both a borough and market town, doing a considerable trade with the inhabitants of the Island. It was most probably founded by the Romans as a port to the then capital, Carisbrooke, and was called Meda. It received its first Charter from Richard de Redvers in the reign of Henry II. It now holds fifteen Charters from various British

monarchs. The town is surrounded by lofty downs. High Street, the principal road of the town, is a part of the main road through the Island from Yarmouth to Ryde. St. Thomas's Church was originally built in 1172, and was dedicated to Thomas à'Beckett. It was pulled down in 1853 and the present structure erected. The foundation stone was laid in 1854 by the late Prince Consort, in the presence of the Queen and her court.

WHIPPINGHAM.

About three miles from Newport is Whippingham. The village itself is of considerable antiquity, its name appearing in the Domesday Book. The Church was founded by William Fitz-Osborne in 1066; the present Church was designed by Albert, Prince Consort, and rebuilt by Queen Victoria, in conjunction with him, in 1851. It was at Whippingham Church that Princess Beatrice and Prince Henry of Battenburg were married. The Royal Family attend the services when in residence at Osborne. Within a short distance is

OSBORNE HOUSE.

Osborne. It was here that Queen Victoria spent the greater part of her time when in England, and where she ultimately passed away, January 22nd, 1901.
The Palace is in the Italian domestic style of architecture; it is fireproof throughout. The roofs are flat, and, being paved with stone, form a delightful promenade. The gardens are tastefully laid out in terraces, bright with flowers and ornamented with sculpture and fountains. During the King's stay at Cowes a Royal yacht lies here and a man-of-war is stationed in the roadstead.

QUEEN VICTORIA IN HER GARDEN CARRIAGE AT OSBORNE, ISLE OF WIGHT.

DRAWING ROOM.
CORRIDOR.

OSBORNE HOUSE.

DINING ROOM,
INDIAN ROOM

NOBLE.
QUEEN VICTORIA'S
FAVOURITE COLLIE.

OSBORNE HOUSE.

QUEEN VICTORIA READING HER MORNING CORRESPONDENCE.
THE BILLIARD ROOM.

IN THE DRAWING ROOM.
THE INDIAN ROOM.

THE R.Y. SQUADRON SLIPWAY COWES.

THE FLOATING BRIDGE & ROYAL LANDING STAGE E. COWES.

THE RIVER MEDINA & EAST COWES.

MARINE PARADE WEST COWES.

We now cross the River Medina by the floating bridge to West Cowes, the El Dorado ot yachtsmen. At the western extremity of the Parade is West Cowes Castle, the headquarters of the Royal Yacht Squadron. Its guns and bastions are used only for saluting the victorious yachts at the annual Regatta (which takes place early in August) and at other peaceful carnivals. The yacht racing has made Cowes famous the world over.

THE VICTORIA PIER, COWES.

This Pier, opened in the Spring of 1902, makes a great addition to the many attractions of Cowes. It offers facilities for the berthing of the largest excursion steamers, and will undoubtedly be a great boon to the town. It is quite modern in design, and while light and elegant in appearance is yet built sufficiently strong to withstand the action of the wind and waves in the roughest weather. A little to the west of the Pier is the Royal Landing Stage, used by the King when visiting Cowes.

THE MARINE PARADE, COWES.

The Parade, which of late has been greatly improved, affords a grand view across the Solent. During the yachting season, for about half a mile either way east and west, the yachts, steam pinnaces, and boats, darting to and fro, form such a gay spectacle as can seldom be witnessed elsewhere.

At the west end of the Parade is the Club House of the Royal Yacht Squadron. The vessels of members are admitted into all foreign ports free of harbour dues.

NEW PARADE

MARINE PARADE

COWES GREEN

West Cowes, the Green of which was handsomely presented to the town by G. H. Stephenson, Esq., in 1863, and laid out as a recreation ground, enclosed by posts and chains, and liberally provided with seats. It is ornamented with a drinking fountain and a number of statues. St. Mary's Church was built in 1658, and, in accordance with the Puritanical Spirit of the times, was not then dedicated to any saint. In 1867-68 it was pulled down and rebuilt. It was then it received its present name. Trinity Church was built in 1831-32 at the cost of Mrs. Goodwin, who endowed it with £1000 in the Consols. It is of the pointed Gothic style of architecture, and fitted up in a tasteful and appropriate manner

Leaving the Green and the Parade, passing through Bath Street into High Street (which is the commercial part of the town), on the left-hand side, about half-way up, is the Pontoon, from which we can embark on one of the South of England Royal Mail Steam Packet Company's steamers, which leave several times daily, and in less than one and a half hours once again reach the mainland having enjoyed a happy holiday in the Isle of Wight.

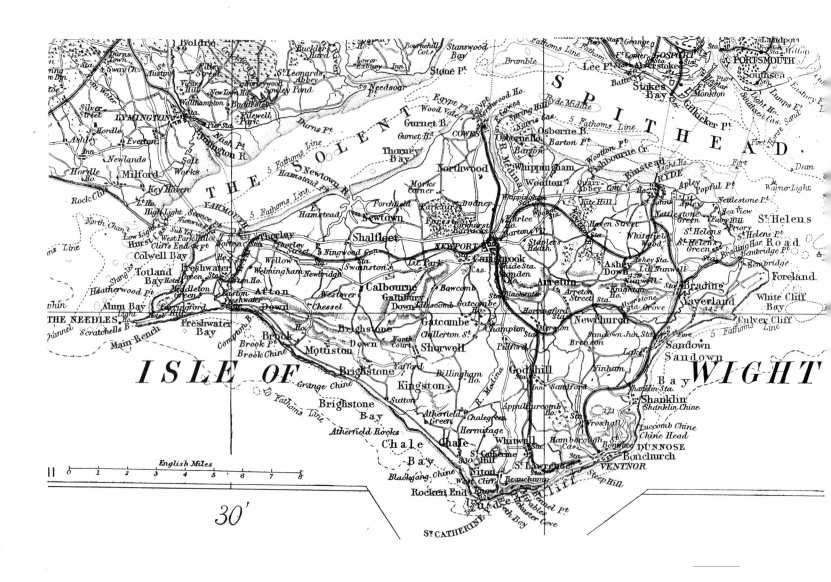